HOW TO TURN YOUR PAIN INTO GAIN

INI NTOLMA

HOW TO TURN YOUR PAIN INTO GAIN

WRITTEN BY
INI NTOLMA
inintolma@gmail.com

ISBN: 978-978-799-596-9

Published by:

COMMUNE WRITERS INT'L
www.communewriters.com
+234 8139 260 389
6, Amusa Street, Agodo-Egbe, Lagos

Published in the Federal Republic of Nigeria

CONTENTS

INTRODUCTION

Have you ever experienced a pain so great that it grips your heart and wouldn't let go or allow you to think properly?

Sometimes, we feel we are in the worst situations, so we wallow in self-pity and wear sad faces all day. But listen, although the story I will share with you may sound worse, some people have been in worst situations than either yours or mine. There are people with stories worse than yours.

In this book, we are not going to dwell on our pains or past, rather, we will discuss how to leverage and turn them into wealth.

Change, they say, begins with you. In other words, if you desire a change, you must be ready to change.

You may suddenly become a single mother like I did on the 22nd of September, 2019. Do you then wallow in self-pity or entertain negative thoughts? No! You have to embrace the change and work selflessly to keep going.

This book is for you. It's for every widow and single mother who suddenly finds herself in this unexpected situation and feel like giving up. It is also for everyone who thinks the world is against him. By reading this book, you are on the right path.

I decided to embrace the situation I found myself. Everything I did from the day my husband breathe his last till today, which has helped me live with three kids, is what I am going to share in this book.

You deciding to read this book means you desire a change, want to overcome your situation, stay afloat, and become a storyteller or a counsellor tomorrow.

This book is not fictional but contains life experiences put together to encourage you to stay positive and live happily.

My life changed when I intentionally applied the lessons in this book and I believe yours will also be a testimony as you apply the lessons.

If you are ready, let's dive in.

CHAPTER ONE

CHOOSE POSITIVITY

My life took a new turn the day I discovered the power of a positive mindset.

The major asset you have, which can help you stand tall amidst challenges, is your mind.

It's not possible to feed your mind with a good meal and not experience growth on the outside.

I got married happily in 2012 at my desired age. I was the first to be married legally and traditionally in my family. So, I was counted lucky. After a short time, my husband's health started deteriorating. My little world was shattered as we were in and out of the hospital, spending our earnings on drugs and medical treatments. Happiness jumped out of the window and we were left with misery. I woke up in the early hours of September 22nd, 2019 to the worst news of my life. From the moment I watched my husband breathe his last and was taken from my hands by the mortuary attendants, I made up my mind to work on myself; to live for the responsibilities ahead and the destinies attached to mine.

Immediately, I started working on my mind not to accept the current situation.

No matter the situation you find yourself, if it hasn't affected your mind, then you can overcome and rise again. A person can be blind, lame or deaf, and function well regardless, but once the mind is tampered with, it's over. Such a person would likely act worse than an animal. The mind is the engine of every human.

Like Robin Sharma said, "Until you are great internally, you cannot be great outside."

I chose to be great internally.

What did I do to overcome this situation and keep my mind positive? Amid grief, while being surrounded by sympathizers, I sneaked out to a bookshop and picked some books. While people came to console me, I preached to them and entertained them with my humour. I was intentional about staying positive and casting out fear about the future. I listened to audio sermons and researched people who overcame tough situations. I listened to their testimonies and I worked and I am still working daily on staying positive. I nicknamed myself; "Mrs Positive Mindset."

It's a daily fight. You shouldn't relent in your effort to stay positive.

Until you have a positive mindset, you cannot see the brightness of each day.

As Gary Zukav puts it, "Positive emotions empower; negative emotions disempower."

Each day comes with numerous opportunities and it takes only a bright mind to see those opportunities.

To stay positive means to be happy in any situation and expect things to work for your good. If you believe that a situation, no matter how ugly or unpleasant, will turn out in your favour, then so shall it be.

Jesus Christ told the people before healing them, "According to your belief ..." What you believe and what you expect has a lot to do with what will manifest.

Having a positive mindset boils down to your belief.

You have to believe that you will make it and that you are not alone. You have to believe that you are not a failure. You have to believe that all hope is not lost.

You have to believe that widowhood is not synonymous with disability and it's not the end of life.

You have to believe that your kids are not punishments but blessings.

You have to believe that you are only a steward and that the owner of those kids cannot let them starve to death.

You have to believe the promises of God such as in Psalms 34:10: "The young lions do lack, and suffer hunger: but they that seek the LORD shall not want any good thing."

I wrote out this portion of the Bible, pasted it on my kitchen wall and declared it every morning.

Believe the promises of God; search for them, write them out and keep them within your sight.

A belief system is a powerful tool, capable of making an ant look like an elephant and an elephant seem like an ant.

People's thought and beliefs are what make them see circumstances differently.

You have to believe that as a widow and a single mother, it is not yet over.

You have to think positively and discard every belief that is not in your favour.

Joyce Meyer advises, "If remembering something from the past is going to help you, then recall it but if it is going to hurt, it is useless recalling it."

The way you see things makes all the difference.

David and his brothers saw an obstacle but from different points of view.

While his brothers saw a giant, David saw an ant and this helped him in going after Goliath.

When you see your situation as a giant, it's going to weigh you down. But if you can view it in a different light, then it will not weigh you down.

Remember, nothing can stop a determined woman.

There's so much power embedded in a woman. This makes the devil afraid of women. You have to know and use that power to your advantage.

If your beliefs are positive, you will always seek valuable lessons from everything that happens to you, both the ugly and the beautiful, and that will help you move to greater heights.

I made a decision long ago that nothing will ever bring me down as long as I live. If it doesn't take my life, then there's a lesson to take home from it.

Having such a mindset makes you develop fast because you are learning while also expecting something positive from everything.

Napoleon Hill said, "Within every difficulty or obstacle, there is a seed of an equal or greater advantage or benefit."

Seek to see the advantage of your present condition. I am sure that with a positive mindset, you will see the advantages in your situation.

Remember, as a man thinketh in his heart, so is he.

What you believe is what you get.

Brian Tracy said, "You do not believe what you see; you see what you already believe."

Your focus from now on should be to entertain beliefs that will aid your growth and discard all self-limiting mindsets. That's what I am here to help you achieve.

When one electric bulb is in use, its level of brightness cannot be compared to when two or three bulbs are being used together.

I am here to work with you as a bulb, to add my light to yours. I pray that as you read on about how I survived with my kids and others who survived tough times, you will be motivated to live happily and take good care of your kids.

Until you listen to your neighbor's story, you would think your case is the worst. I thought I was too young to be a widow until I came across widows younger than I am. I thought I was in a worse scenario until I heard the worst stories. You may never appreciate God until you hear about the next person's experience.

There's so much you can achieve if you remain positive and always enthusiastic.

CHAPTER TWO

YOU ARE NOT A VICTIM

This chapter is going to complement the previous chapter. It will prepare your mind to understand the messages on subsequent pages.

You become a victim when you think you are a victim. For as a man thinketh in his heart, so is he (Proverbs 23:7).

Having a victim mentality will make you mediocre all the days of your life.

I am here to remind you that you are not a victim. The earlier you accept this, the better. Tell your subconscious mind that you are a victor and that you are blessed.

My mindset changed in 2016 when I watched a program organised by the Governor of Lagos State at the time, for physically-challenged citizens. It was the State's anniversary but it was organised to celebrate the physically challenged and as such, they came out in their numbers to display their talents. I was moved to tears as I saw the blind, lame, people with Down syndrome and others, making use of their talents while I was whole but could do nothing with such a privilege.

I went home that day and decided to pay attention to myself. I asked myself, "Ini, what can you do with your eyes, nose, legs, hands and the beautiful life you have?"

Until you demand answers, you cannot get one.

It's time to discard that victim mentality and take full advantage of your body parts.

If you are widowed, you still have a life to live. The fact that you're alive despite everything, means you have the chance to be useful and productive. Look within and bring out the best.

You are a divorcee, not a victim. You're still living. So, take advantage of it.

If you had a child out of wedlock, he/she is a blessing. You are not a victim.

Believing you are not a victim is one of the strategies to move to a higher level in life.

I do not want you to finish this chapter without realizing how privileged you are to be alive and then decide to live it to the fullest.

Until you discard the victim mentality, you cannot be happy.

And until you live a happy life, you cannot see the opportunities life will bring your way.

It takes a positive mind to recognize opportunities.

Stop fuming and blaming others for the situation you're in.

If you keep blaming others, life will continue to be difficult for you.

I remember my first year as a single mother and a widow. I was embittered because people were not helping me. I was angry with my in-laws, friends, the church and my late husband's friends.

The more I got angry, the more frustrated I became.

I couldn't recognize what God was doing for me and the kids because I was busy blaming others and expecting everybody to help me.

As long as you are expecting help from others, you will remain a victim because you will always want to appear pathetic to gain their sympathy.

Victim mentality will make you dress, walk, talk and behave like a victim to attract pity. It's a miserable lifestyle.

That shouldn't be your position.

You know what? Great things only follow great minds while inferior things follow inferior minds. You have to work on your mind to attract great and beautiful things.

Change can only come from the inside. Once you are angry within and demand a change, things will change on the outside.

My mindset changed when I told myself, "Ini, these people you are expecting help from, also have their problems and they don't owe you anything."

Everybody needs help and God is the only one who can help all of us. No one owes you.

You have to wake up, brace up, dress up and fight to live to the fullest. That decision should happen right now. Decide to no longer look like a victim.

As a man thinketh in his heart, so is he.

You know what?

You cannot raise your kids to live like beggars.

How you choose to live will also affect their lifestyle, so I urge you to live like a winner.

You deserve the good things in life but you have to be mentally prepared for it.

You can't live your life depending on others. You too can help others.

You can't be stagnant because waiting for others to help brings stagnation.

Successful people do not just walk into success. They work their way into it, with their thoughts, beliefs, attitudes, appearance, and everything.

You only attract your kind. Once you discard the victim mentality and start thinking like a winner, you will attract good things. When you walk, talk, dress and behave like a winner, you'll begin to feel like a winner and in no time, your association will change, the kind of opportunities you come across will change and your life will change too.

So, it must begin with you, from within.

Remember, looking like a victim will only attract peanuts from people and some might take advantage of you. So, brace up and reset your mind.

A story was shared of a sales manager who always takes his newly employed salesmen to a car dealership. He would force them to sell their old cars and buy them the latest cars. With this, the new salesmen were forced to act in line with their new level. Their attitude towards themselves began to change. They began to see themselves as the type that can own the latest cars and earn big salaries. Thereafter, this mindset affected their sales. They began to think big and as such, began to earn more.

Nothing changes until your mind changes.

You need to have a mental image of yourself so that when it becomes a reality, you will be proud of yourself.

Don't play the victim. Since you become what you think, you should think of greatness only. Remind yourself daily that you are a winner. Declare it until your subconscious mind accepts it.

Believe, speak and see.

CHAPTER THREE

YOUR PRIORITY

Nothing works until you are committed to it.

As a single mother, your focus and priority should be on raising your kids to make you proud tomorrow.

You cannot benefit from what you are not committed to.

Your kids being the utmost priority will guide your decisions.

Every minute you invest in your kids is like a seed. It would germinate and bear fruits.

I once ran into a post on social media where a young man was seeking counsel. His mother was a widow and her late husband was wealthy.

After two years of his demise, his 52-year-old mother found love again with a poor widower and she got carried away. She neglected the children and squandered her late husband's money on her newfound love. The children kept wondering if their mother was charmed or still in her right senses.

In this scenario, she has lost all respect before those children.

As a single mother, you are vulnerable to men. You need wisdom in all you do and remember, every action will either make or mar you. Things will happen but your response will determine what comes next.

Challenges will either move you forward or backwards. It depends on your response to your current challenge.

Every action has its consequence.

If you must reap, you must sow.

Once again, your children are watching and learning from you. You are their number one role model. You will read more about this on the next page.

You can indirectly or ignorantly mislead them.

It is a common belief that children from single mothers don't amount to anything in life. But you have to make a decision like I did, to change that narrative.

It starts with your relationship with them. It starts with what they see you do daily.

It starts with what they hear you say and how you respond to issues.

The best way to get kids to do something is not by telling them but by showing them how it's done.

If I want my kids to be prayerful, I should be prayerful myself. They should always see me praying. With that, my persuasiveness will be reduced.

Make them your priority and let all your decisions revolve around God and them.

CHAPTER FOUR

WHAT CAN YOU SEE?

"Whether you are a success or a failure, it has little to do with your circumstances; it has much to do with your choices" - ***Nido Qubein***

The circumstance you find yourself is not the problem, it is rather, in how you see that circumstance. Two people can face the same problem and come out of it in different ways due to their perception of the problem. One person can go on to become better, while the other might come off worse than he already was. It all depends on how you see and perceive a problem. So I ask, what do you see?

If you see an overwhelming situation, you would be overwhelmed.

One truth I have discovered is that God never closes a door without opening another. But often, we stay and stare regretfully at the closed door and fail to notice a new one that has been opened for us.

As for me, no matter the condition, it is for my good. I have a positive attitude towards any condition I find myself and it has been helping me in overcoming challenges. I see every encounter as an opportunity for growth.

Successful people look for the good in every situation. They believe every setback is part of a great plan to move them towards achieving their goals. When you set out with this mindset, you would keep winning.

Myles Munroe says, "Sight restricts you to the present."

Are you being limited by your sight or can you see beyond it?

You can acquire as far as you can see.

And I ask again, what can you see from where you are standing?

Your vision will give you hope and a purpose but if you are limited to what's within your sight, you would be miserable.

Sight is the function of your eyes while vision is the function of your mind. You have to allow your mind to travel far.

The way people see things is what makes them view the same circumstance differently.

John Maxwell in one of his books; Failing Forward, says, "Creativity is being able to see what everybody else has seen and think what nobody else has thought, so that you can do what nobody else has done."

See your troubles as blessings, resolve to transform your stumbling blocks into stepping stones and turn your wounds into wisdom.

David saw Goliath as an ant while his brothers saw him as a giant. How you respond to your situation depends on how you see it.

If you must succeed, you have to see things in a way that would favour you and not in a way that would limit your growth.

That's why the Bible teaches in Luke 11:34, "Your eyes are like a lamp for the body. When your eyes are sound, your whole body is full of light; but when your eyes are no good, your whole body will be put in darkness."

How you see things determines how you respond.

If you train your eyes to see God's blessings amid adversaries, I tell you, your whole body will be sound and you will be able to function well.

I told you how I dealt with widowhood in the previous chapter.

Initially, I joined many widowhood groups online but I couldn't cope psychologically. It made me feel miserable and disadvantaged. I woke up one day and exited all the groups.

If you must succeed, you have to be in an environment that would help you succeed.

Be in an environment where others are striving to succeed. When you are exposed to success and other people's achievements, you would be challenged to do better.

Two people can experience the same thing but respond differently. The difference is in how they see the situation.

My prayer is that as you are reading this book, you will decide to see a better picture of yourself and your future. Until you see, you can't acquire.

There's a story of two men who were sent from their company in China to carry out a survey in Africa. They were to check if there would be a market for the sale of footwear.

Let me call them Sam and Dick.

When they arrived, Sam and Dick saw that people don't wear shoes in Africa. Everybody was walking barefoot.

Sam was very excited to have found a market for the business while Dick was frustrated because people don't wear shoes.

Sam went back, discussed with the company, signed a deal with them and started manufacturing shoes for sale in Africa. He became a millionaire while Dick remained poor because he couldn't see the opportunity.

You have to train your eyes to see opportunities in every situation. Your eyes are like a lamp for your body.

With your present state, what can you see about yourself in the next few months?

People who have climbed the ladder of success today, have imagined themselves climbing it. They have pictured themselves in that position mentally before they got there physically.

All the things you see on the streets were once mental images in people's heads. So I ask, what can you see?

You need to have a big mental image of yourself and work with it because you would be pulled in the direction of your thought.

If you do not have a mental image of where you want to be, life will dump you anywhere.

You can never go higher than your vision. The limit of your faith in your vision is the limit of your achievement.

Never limit yourself with your thoughts. Allow your mind to travel far.

Imagine yourself in a better position than your current status.

Imagine yourself in a better apartment than your current apartment.

Don't be like the prodigal son's elder brother in the book of Luke. Don't rob yourself. All the good things in life are already here and are yours. Don't settle for less. Don't be afraid to enjoy. Don't transfer it to others. You too can be a partaker.

Life hasn't cheated you; you cheat yourself with your mindset. I tell my kids daily, "don't be intimidated, you are the best and the best place belongs to you." When you have a healthy mindset, you will see beyond your physical eyes. That's why the Bible urges us to live by faith and not by sight. Sight limits your achievement and keeps you stagnant but faith allows you to fly. So, live by faith and fly with faith.

CHAPTER FIVE

EMBRACE CHANGE

"It's impossible to grow without a change"

- John Mason

Many people want their situation to change but are not ready to change themselves and are not ready to embrace change.

You cannot become what you are destined to be by remaining who you have been. Changing your life starts by changing your mind and what you do in your mind will manifest on the outside.

John Patterson says, “Only fools and dead men don’t change their minds.”

It’s time to change the way you do things if you must experience a change.

“Those who cannot change their minds cannot change anything” - John Mason.

You have remained where you are for so long because of a fixed belief system. Every belief is supposed to help you grow and if it’s not, then it’s time to let it go.

Before I took the decision that change my life, everything was ugly because of my mindset.

I stayed awake one night and asked myself what I could do to change my situation. With a look at my beautiful kids, I decided to be responsible for my life.

Oprah Winfrey says, “If you are not in the driver’s seat of your life, life will drive you.”

I sat and wrote down things I was going to do from that moment on to change my life. I started from my mindset down to daily affirmations and actions.

I cut a piece of paper, drew a line and wrote the things I was going to be doing to help my mind on the right with blue ink and the things I was going to stop doing on the left with red ink. That had a good effect on my life till now.

When you change, many people will complain; but if you have a good reason for changing, stick to it. They will appreciate it as you grow.

It's time to change your environment.

It's time to change your associations. You will see more about this in the next chapter.

It's time to change the way you reason.

It's time to love and stop waiting to be loved. It's time to give and stop waiting to receive. You know it's more blessed to give than to receive.

It's time to do something different from what you have been doing.

Take a look at social media apps like Facebook. How many times have they changed, so they can grow and make more profit?

When Facebook came in, there was no room for editing posts, but they kept adding different features to serve people better.

When you are static, with the same old pattern of thinking and belief, can you grow? It's impossible to grow that way.

You have to learn something that you haven't learned to fit into the ever-changing environment. Open up to learning.

Unlearn the junks you have learned and give room for new knowledge.

Herbert Spencer adds that, "A living thing is distinguished from the dead by the multiplicity of the changes at any moment taking place in it."

If you ever want things to change for you, if you want to experience a new life, then it's time for you to change.

Take a look at your environment. Is it helping you to think big? Is there anything to challenge your growth in that environment? If not, then it's time to change your environment.

When I lost my husband in 2019, I knew there was no way I could continue living in an environment where people would be wearing pitiable faces whenever they see me. No, I couldn't stand that. The first step to my growth was to change my environment.

Your target is to grow and be a blessing to your generation. Therefore, anything that would make you remember your ugly past and limit your growth should be avoided.

The way to live a happy and productive life is to have peace of mind by eliminating people, situations and environment that makes you unhappy.

Remember, your response to what happens will determine your outcome. For your life to face a new direction if you don't like where you are now and what you are seeing, you have to change your thinking pattern and mindset.

The four lepers in 2 Kings 7:3 needed a change. They came to their senses and acted fast.

The prodigal son also needed a change in his situation and the Bible recorded that he came to his senses, took a decision and what followed was a change.

If you need a change in your situation, you must rise and act but if you are afraid to take a step, then you are afraid of growth.

Those who are slow in decision-making are those who are slow in growth.

When you think right, then you will act right.

John Maxwell says, "Achievement comes from the habit of good thinking."

You can continue in your old ways but you can never get anything new from it.

I urge you to think better so you can live better.

This is what I want you to do.

Make a list of things you could change in your life right now. What don't you like around you?

List the steps you can take to change those things. Once you are determined to change them, you will find a way out.

John Maxwell said, "If you want to live on a new level, you have to think on a new level."

Think only about the things you want to see and you will attract them in no time. When an idea drops, be fast to act on the instructions because ideas are fleeting.

Don't drag your feet any longer. Act fast and grow. Anything you don't like, move to change it.

CHAPTER SIX

ASSOCIATE RIGHT

"I just do not hang around anybody that I don't want to be with. Period. For me, that's been a blessing, and I can stay positive. I hang around happy people, who are growing, who want to learn, who don't mind saying sorry or thank you, and are having a fun time"

- John Assaraf

You are better off spending time alone than spending time with people who will hold you back with their victim mentality and their mediocrity.

Confidence is contagious, and so is lack of confidence. You cannot surround yourself with cowards and expect to be better.

In the previous chapter, I told you how I exited widowhood groups because I needed to be sane. I needed an environment where I could learn and grow. I needed an environment where I would be challenged to be the best and one where I would be taught to be dependent. Bad things happen but what you make out of it matters. When you are in a crisis, you need a good environment to think of the way forward. Good circumstances with bad friends result in defeat but bad circumstances with good friends result in victory.

Being a widow or single mother does not mean you are paralyzed or disabled. Failure in business does not mean you cannot succeed in anything else. You are only a failure if you fail and refuse to get up. You have a functional brain, hands, legs, eyes and everything that can help you succeed if you are ready to use them.

Jack Canfield says in his book, The Success Principles, that, "Success is not reserved just for those born into well-to-do families, without challenges, or to whom every advantage has been given."

Success is for those who have the right mindset and are working towards a goal.

If you have a vision, why waste time in an environment that won't help you to achieve your goals?

Every step should be towards achieving your life goal. If your association is not helping you grow, what are you doing in their midst?

It's very important to spend time with the people we want to be like.

I love Oprah Winfrey and what she represents and I place her picture where I can be seeing it daily because we become what we look at.

You must make everything work for your good.

Charles Jones says, "What you are today is what you will be in five years except for two things; the people with whom you associate and the books you read."

If your mission is to grow and fulfil your purpose, then you must look for people who are growing.

There's a story of a baby lion who was playing while his mother slept one day. As different objects caught his attention, the cub thought he could explore a bit and see what the world looks like beyond his home. He kept going and before he realized it, he had gone far and couldn't find his way home.

Stranded and afraid, he wandered everywhere and, in every direction, calling piteously for his mother but got no response. He didn't know what to do until he came across a sheep whose offspring had been taken away from her. Hearing his cries, the sheep made friends with him, consoled and adopted him.

The sheep became his new companion and she grew very fond of him. In a short time, the cub had grown so large that the sheep became afraid of his size. They kept living together happily until one day when a magnificent lion appeared from the top of a hill. He roared and it echoed throughout the hills.

The sheep trembled and was paralyzed with fear. But the moment the sound reached the cub's ears, he was spellbound and started feeling strange.

The lion's roar aroused a force within him which had never been awoken. Without a thought about what he was doing, he answered the lion's call with a corresponding roar.

Trembling with fear, surprised and bewildered at such power, the cub gave his foster mother, the sheep, a pathetic look and then, with a tremendous leap, started running towards the lion on the hill.

The lion has found his lost self. He had discovered himself. Before this time, he was living as though he was a lamb, and never dreamt of doing things that his companion could not do or thought he had more strength than a sheep. He never imagined that there was a power within him which would bring terror to the beasts of the jungle. He simply thought he was a sheep and would run at the sight of a dog or a wolf. Now, he was surprised to see the dogs, wolves, and other animals flee from him.

As long as he was with the sheep and thought he was a sheep, he walked like a sheep, was timid and reserved like a sheep, and had only a sheep's strength and courage.

The roar of the lion didn't add any new power to him. It only aroused the power that has been dormant in him as a result of his association and environment. The roar simply revealed to him the kind of power he had.

This is exactly what happens to anyone staying in the wrong environment. There's a sleeping lion in you that needs just a roar from another lion to awaken it and stir you up. There is probably a longing in your spirit which needs a lion's roar to come alive.

I never knew I could speak in public until the day I was called to do so. One day, as I was returning from work, I saw an advert for a seminar. My soul clung to it and I decided to attend. From the first day of that event, the host fell in love with my personality and on the last day of the program, he asked me to anchor the event. I panicked initially and told him I had not done such before. He replied, "Ini, you can." I summoned courage and accepted the offer. That event exposed a part of me I never knew existed. I fell in love with the microphone and it has been like that till today. Being around people who were hungry for growth stirred the sleeping lion in me.

As long as you are hanging around with the sheep, you will think like a sheep and will never improve on your skills and knowledge. When you associate with people higher than you, you start thinking like them.

John Maxwell said, "You can only learn if others are ahead of you."

I have always associated with people higher than me, so I can learn from them.

If you surround yourself with chicken-minded people, you become chicken-minded too. No matter how clean the water is, once a drop of dirt enters, it becomes contaminated. Bad company will only lead you to bad places. Firstly, you have to know where you are going, to know the kind of people to associate with.

Proverbs 27:19 says, "A mirror reflects a man's face, but what he is really like is shown by the kind of friends he chooses."

If all your friends do is lament and talk about past losses, how people have not been helping, how to follow men and the number of men they have, you are going down a tunnel.

You must be intentional about whom you associate with if you will make progress in life and be a blessing to your kids and the world at large.

This book has been on my computer for long. I had been dragging my feet in completing it until I attended the 2022 International Women's Day Conference and caught the fire. I rose to complete this book for you.

There's power bestowed in you and you just need a good environment and companions to stir that out. It's time to look within you to bring out that natural gift. If harnessed, it can cater for your family's needs.

I already captured the vision for my life long ago and that helped me to stand in the face of adversity. My vision helped me in making choices, including the choice of friends. People who do not walk with a vision can easily fall during adversity and never rise again. But if you have a vision, it strengthens you to keep going.

I will end this chapter by saying, look at your closest association. It's an indication of the direction you are going.

CHAPTER SEVEN

HOW TO DEVELOP A HEALTHY SELF-ESTEEM

"Love yourself first and everything else will fall in line"

- Lucille Ball

Many of the things we do daily result from how we perceive ourselves.

Self-esteem is about how much you appreciate and like yourself. It's an individual's overall evaluation of her worth.

The fact that Christ came for your sake speaks of how valuable you are. You are not defined by your circumstances or material possessions. You are the best from creation. Each of us was built to win in life.

A diva is always a diva, whether broken or thriving, wealthy or poor. To be great, having this mindset is important because greatness is an inward event with an outward result. It's a result of what is happening within you. If you rise to a world-class level in your thoughts, feelings and behaviour, then you will be a world-class person.

Your self-esteem is determined by your self-image; how you see yourself.

I gave you an example of a lion and a sheep in the previous chapter. As long as the lion saw himself as a sheep, he continued to act like a sheep. The way you see yourself determines the things you do, how you do them, and the things you accept from people.

Your self-image guides your behaviour. The moment you replace low self-esteem with a grander image of yourself, feelings of inferiority and self-pity behaviours will cease.

You behave the way you do because you haven't seen yourself the way God sees you.

It's low self-esteem that makes you dress, talk and live the way you do, which is not healthy for you and your kids.

It's low self-esteem that makes you accept ill-treatment from people.

When you develop healthy self-esteem, you will begin to act like the queen that you are.

John Maxwell says, "We can do very few things in a positive way if we feel negative about ourselves."

Yes, you are a widow or a single mother, but you are still valuable. And you must see this, starting from your mind. If you value yourself, you will carry yourself with poise and command respect from others. The way people treat you comes from how you treat yourself.

When you see yourself as the best, you act with more strength and personal power.

Superior people have a clear and grand image of who they are; they believe in themselves. No one will treat you right until you treat yourself right. Whenever you decide that things must change, things will begin to change.

Some Israelites were sent to spy on the promised land. When they got there and saw the occupants of the land, they trembled and came back with an intimidating report. They had a wrong picture of themselves. They saw themselves as ants and there was nothing they could achieve with such a mindset. Thank God for Joshua who had a clear image of himself and his brothers. He corrected them immediately. He spurred them into action and that was how they conquered.

Having a wrong mental image of yourself will keep you on the ground forever.

Inferior thoughts come from a wrong self-image.

All that the New Testament is trying to teach and buttress to us is our real image. The New Testament tried to show us our real identity. Men who are succeeding today are those who have grabbed that real identity of themselves in Christ Jesus.

You cannot live a world-class life by having inferior thoughts. You must continually declare who you are.

I made a list of adjectives about myself and pasted it by my bedside where I can always see.

I declare them always so that my subconscious mind can absorb them and signal them to all my senses.

Right thinking gives birth to right choices and right choices give birth to better results and a better life.

If you desire to become a champion in life like me, you must see yourself as a champion before you can begin to think and behave like one. A high-quality life starts with high-quality thoughts and a high-quality you. Start loving and investing in yourself. You can't wait for anybody to do that for you. Like I earlier said, until you love yourself, no one will love you. Until you appreciate yourself, no one will. Start seeing yourself as the most beautiful and precious person on earth because that's who you are. You start attracting good things and good people when you take care of yourself. Start speaking with authority. Take ownership of yourself. To feel more satisfied, help others. People like to be around nice, lively and lovely people. Think of what will make someone want to see you again.

Think of what will make people look forward to having a conversation with you. Let your presence make people feel better. Yes, you can. It starts with self-love.

You cannot move on in life by carrying baggage from the past. The only way forward is to drop them and focus on what makes you happy and productive.

When I lost my husband, it took a lot of work to recover and be a better person. I studied, listened to messages, and watched videos of other great women. I was battling with low self-esteem. I learned that one way to boost your self-esteem is to add value to others. So I asked myself, "What can I do?"

I remembered I could speak and teach. Immediately, I formed a WhatsApp group where I taught singles how to find a partner and have a good marriage. That was how 360° Relationship Impact was founded amid confusion. The more those single ladies appreciated my work, the more my self-esteem went up. In a bid to add more value, I wrote my first book; HOW TO BE A MORE ATTRACTIVE LADY. I continually wrote on social media to add value to people and as people read and liked my write-ups, I was seeing my value and my self-esteem increased.

Two things happen when you face a crisis. You either become better than you were or worse than you were.

My prayer is that you will become better.

Improving yourself guarantees a future filled with possibilities. The easiest way to boost your self-esteem is to be a blessing to someone. Think of what you can do. Think of what can make you happy. Think of ways to add value to others. When you cause others to smile, you will start seeing yourself as important. I love writing and reading my books gives me joy. So whenever I feel miserable, I write and look for people who need encouragement. While encouraging others and they are appreciating me, I see reasons why I shouldn't give up.

Focus on being better within. The stronger you are inside, the stronger you will be outside.

Robert Schuller in his book, Tough Times Don't Last but Tough People Do, says, "There will never be another you, make the most of yourself."

Life is not a rehearsal. This is your time to manifest what you came to the earth with. Without a positive self-image, you will manifest nothing. Rather, you will return to God with all the potential He has given you.

Create an image of what you want to achieve and hold it firm. In no time, it will become a physical reality.

My journey to being a public speaker and an author began in 2015 after my National Youth Service Corps. Completion of NYSC is one of the most frustrating phases of a Nigerian youth's life. I sat and asked myself questions. I took full stock of my strengths and weaknesses. The result is what you are seeing today.

Have a good image of yourself, believe in your ideas and believe you can become what you desire. Remember, the quickest way to creating a better life is to focus on becoming better. Prosperity starts from within and flows outside. Above all, trust God your creator, who is in charge of the world.

CHAPTER EIGHT

DISCOVER YOUR UNIQUENESS

Every man comes into the world with a special gift and a personality that makes him unique.

True beauty manifests when you identify your real nature and live it to the fullest.

You may feel you are alone but I want to point you to your uniqueness.

You are different from the next person and it comes from your personality and gifts. There are certain things you do with ease that others struggle to do. I want you to pay attention to that and capitalize on it. When you identify and become very good at it, you will eventually be well-paid to do it.

Don't worry about what you cannot do, rather, pay attention to what you can do.

The book of Proverbs says the gift of a man maketh rich. God didn't create us empty. He coupled us with abilities suitable for our calling.

Be assured that the ability is already there. All you need to do is to discover it and sharpen it, so you can be an expert in that area.

If you love cooking, give it a try. How about learning how to do it in a better and bigger way? How about turning it into a business and having fun doing what you love?

If you love to put pieces together to bring out something beautiful, you can learn more about it.

Maybe you love writing like me. Once it's a natural gift, nothing can stand against you. The ability is always there.

It's time to examine yourself.

Pay attention to yourself and ask yourself questions.

I sat down a few years after my NYSC and took a full assessment of myself.

I wrote down my strengths and weaknesses.

I wrote down what I have passion for.

I wrote down the things I do naturally and continuously. And I asked myself, “What can I achieve and how can I serve humanity with these?”

Those questions brought me to where I am today.

Those questions brought about this book and other ones you’ll be reading from me.

I was teaching in a private Secondary School during the COVID-19 lockdown. There was no pay since the school was closed for three months. It was then I looked within and asked myself, “Ini, what can you offer to feed these kids?” I took advantage of my laptop and Android phone and started writing. I already had a platform on WhatsApp where I write to the singles daily. I used my phone, turned all those counsels into an e-book and reached out to someone online who designed a book cover for me. That was how I started advertising the book online and, on my platform, and the singles were ordering for them. I sold the books and used the money to help myself. Plus, my self-esteem increased as a result of that achievement.

Brain Tracy says, "If you want to make more money, become very good at what you do."

People will only pay for the value you can offer.

You can turn your pain into wealth by throwing away the victim mentality to look inward for what you can offer.

You have the power to attract whatever you want but that begins when you take total control of your mind.

Choose what you want to live for.

Choose the name you want to be called.

Choose the path you want to tread and learn everything necessary to become an expert in that field. Once you are ready, the universe will make it happen. All you need now is determination.

My journey to becoming an author and a public speaker began in 2015, after highlighting of all my abilities.

I neglected other opportunities and stayed focused on one goal.

Paul said in Philippians 3:13, "Brethren, I count not myself to have apprehended: but this one thing I do, forgetting those things which are behind, and reaching forth unto those things which are before."

You need to stay focused on the mark for the prize of your high calling.

Your high calling is that yearning in your spirit. It's that special vacuum you were created to fill. No one else has the ability except you.

Discover the vacuum and stay focused on that. Let your name come up whenever people think of anybody in that field.

Now before we end this chapter, I want you to ask yourself these few questions and write your answers on a piece of paper:

✓What can I do with ease?

✓What profession do I admire others doing?

✓What business can I easily do?

✓What natural gift do I possess?

✓What have people been admiring about me?

✓What kind of work can I find fulfilment in?

✓What idea has always been coming to my mind?

✓When I was a kid, what did I dream of becoming?

✓What would I want to change in the world if I have the opportunity?

Answers these questions and see how you can come up with a reasonable path for your life.

As for me, writing and speaking is my path.

There's always something you can do that will make people start looking for you. Examine yourself and bring out that gift.

When you do, refine it and the world will stand at attention for you. Remember, you can't achieve this if your mind is not big enough.

Your achievement starts from your mind. For whatever your mind can conceive, you can achieve.

CHAPTER NINE

HOW TO FIND LOVE AGAIN

The Bible admonishes that women below 60 years of age should not be counted as widows, because it's certain that they would need a companion and are advised to remarry. Even at 60, you can still remarry.

So how can you find love again?

That is the question this chapter is set to answer.

Everything begins with you. It begins with your mindset, words and actions.

For love to find you, you must make up your mind to love again.

You must let go of your past and be ready for a new relationship.

You must make yourself lovely and lovable.

You don't need to take the pains from your previous relationship into the new one, and neither do you need to punish your new partner for the shortcomings of your previous relationship.

You have to rid yourself of every unresolved emotion from past relationships.

No one moves forward while looking back.

The only way to be attractive is to let go of your baggage and take care of yourself. Baggage will weigh you down and make you look pitiable.

You can attract a lover when you love yourself and others.

Step forward to be seen.

Take care of your physical appearance.

As I wrote in my book: HOW TO BE A MORE ATTRACTIVE LADY, your appearance must appeal to the opposite sex before they can come close enough to know how much of a good person you are.

No matter how spiritual a man is, he is attracted by a woman's appearance first, before he notices the inner virtue.

So, you must make your appearance a priority. Smell nice if you want to attract love again.

Secondly, you must position yourself where love can find you. You can't remain in your house all day and expect to find a partner.

Again, you must have a life of your own. Get something to do and be busy doing it. Your work has a way of attracting people to you.

Men don't joke with industrious ladies.

But when you are idle and always demanding, they will take advantage of your idleness.

You don't want to turn yourself into that. For you to be loved and valued, you must get busy. Let a man find you in your place of service and he will value you.

CHAPTER TEN

WIN AND TELL

You would not have a story to tell until you fight your battles. Someone can get encouraged and become mentally stable because of your story one day.

Recently, I see my life story becoming an encouragement to people. I woke up one day to see a message in my inbox from a young man, asking if I was a counselor. I replied, "How may I help you please?" He told me how he had made up his mind to commit suicide because life had been unfair to him. I pleaded with him, but to no avail until I narrated my life history. I told him I am a widow with nothing to hold on to. I told him about all I had gone through in life and he became calm. He gave me a full audience and was even feeling sympathetic for me.

After our conversation, he told me, "Please, can I be a part of your family? Drop your account details, I want to be a part of you." I laughed and told him, "So you had money in your account and you wanted to end your life?"

Oftentimes, the battle you are fighting today is for your journey tomorrow.

The battles you are fighting today would lead you to the next phase of your life.

Like I always say, your response to the challenges of life would determine your next step, either forward or backwards. Things happen, but your response to what happens will determine what will follow.

Until you fight your war, you won't have a story to tell. I urge you to fight and win so that you can tell your story tomorrow.

I can write to you now because I stood firm to fight my war. As the Bible says, no challenge is beyond you and there's nothing new under heaven.

And it says God will make a way out.

You will comfort others tomorrow just as He will comfort you today.

So, stay strong and fight to win.

Be an attacker and not a defender.

Don't play the defensive but be offensive. Play to win.

There's a difference between playing to win and playing defensive.

I urge you to be offensive.

I believe with these, you have seen reasons why you should wake up and live, why you should be grateful for life, and why you should equip your mind.

As your mind is, so are you.

ABOUT THE AUTHOR

Ini Ntolma is a certified relationship counselor, a trainer, self-esteem coach, transformational speaker, Author and a seasoned youth mentor. She is the founder of 360° Relationship Impact, a body that coaches and mentors the singles on relationship and personal development.

She is a graduate of Linguistics from the University of Uyo, Uyo, Akwa Ibom State.

She is a widow and a mother of three lovely kids. She is committed to providing exceptional services to the youths, singles and married and single mothers who are ready to live life to the fullest.

She speaks on the following areas such as Self-discovery, Building self-esteem, Dating and Courtship, Building a successful marriage, Building a personal brand, Life after the Loss of a partner, etc.

www.ingramcontent.com/pod-product-compliance
Lightning Source LLC
LaVergne TN
LVHW090126160826
845673LV00015B/1027

* 9 7 8 9 7 8 7 9 9 5 9 6 9 *